CONTENTS

A NEW HOME TIGER

By Joan Stimson and Meg Rutherford

ABOUT THE SERIES
INSIDE FRONT COVER

BACKGROUND INFORMATION
3–5

LESSON PLANS
6–20

PHOTOCOPIABLES
21–32

SKILLS GRID
INSIDE BACK COVER

CREDITS

Published by Scholastic Ltd,
Villiers House,
Clarendon Avenue,
Leamington Spa,
Warwickshire CV32 5PR
Text © Brenda Williams
© 1999 Scholastic Ltd
1 2 3 4 5 6 7 8 9 0   9 0 1 2 3 4 5 6

Author Brenda Williams
Series consultant Fiona Collins
Editor Clare Gallaher
Assistant editor Roanne Davis
Series designer Lynne Joesbury
Designer Claire Belcher
Illustrations redrawn by Claire Belcher from originals by
Meg Rutherford, by permission of the illustrator;
Illustrations pages 22, 25–27, 29 and 32, Kirsty Wilson
Cover illustration Meg Rutherford

Designed using Adobe Pagemaker

British Library Cataloguing-in-Publication Data
A catalogue record for this book is available from the British Library.

ISBN 0-439-01624-X

BACKGROUND INFORMATION

GENRE

A New Home for Tiger, written by Joan Stimson and beautifully illustrated by Meg Rutherford, is a delightful picture book. The story, about a young tiger moving home, is sensitively told in clear and simple sentences. There are just two main characters, enabling children to empathize closely with Tiger and many of the feelings he experiences as he confronts the change in his life. The illustrations add an extra dimension which amplify and support the emotions suggested in the text, developing a deeper understanding of the story.

PLOT SUMMARY

Tiger is living a happy and carefree life when his mother tells him they are moving house. His initial excitement during the novelty of packing turns to doubt as he finally leaves his old house. He finds the strangeness of his new surroundings unsettling, and seeks reassurance from his mother. Unable to adapt he moves through unhappiness and non-compliance to rebelliousness, when he decides to go back to his old home. Though helped in both moves by a wonderfully amiable elephant who features only in the illustrations, Tiger's joy at returning quickly dissipates and, as the moon goes down and he reaches the empty house, he becomes nervous and fearful. Without the familiarity of his mother, his old home doesn't feel right. Suddenly he realizes that home is more than a building, and he races back. The happy ending is cleverly emphasized in the text by the use of phrases which described his idyllic life at the beginning of the story, and the reader is assured he is once again a cheerful tawny tiger who sleeps like a dormouse.

ABOUT THE AUTHOR

Joan Stimson was brought up in the Midlands and graduated from London University. She then moved to Gloucestershire, where she worked for a number of years in industry and later began writing for children. Joan specializes in picture book texts for the very young, several of which have been illustrated by Meg Rutherford. She is married with two grown-up daughters. Her hobbies include walking, swimming and vintage cars.

ABOUT THE ILLUSTRATOR

Meg Rutherford was brought up on an isolated farm in Australia where books and animals were her natural companions. After leaving school, she went to work as a housekeeper. Her employer, noticing how beautifully she carved wood into chains in her spare time, encouraged her artistic talent and suggested she apply to art college – which she did, studying sculpture at the Slade School in London. But she was always drawing as well as exhibiting – until her first book, *Beautiful Island*, was published. Since then she has illustrated lots of books (and written some of them!). She now lives in Dorset, where one of her favourite activities is walking her little rescue dog, Ferry, by the sea.

SPECIFIC TEACHING OPPORTUNITIES

TEXT LEVEL

The very simplicity of the text of *A New Home for Tiger* enables it, at one level, to be explored and sequenced in a clearly defined structure. It can be read individually, or in a group, and offers opportunities for role-play. At this basic level it lends itself easily to retelling, and review. However, there is another level at which the reader can become immersed. Tiger's *feelings* also follow a sequential path. They are clearly mentioned in the text, and developed and enhanced by the expressive illustrations, enabling groups to consider the reasons for incidents in the story. Children can identify with Tiger and draw comparisons from their own lives, giving opportunities for discussion and written work about situational experiences, both about Tiger and themselves.

SENTENCE LEVEL

Joan Stimson's sentence structure in *A New Home for Tiger* is so clear and straightforward that analysis can be easily and simply presented to children. The text is an ideal vehicle for work on sentence construction and punctuation, enabling children to identify sentences within the text and take account of such features as capitalization at the beginning of sentences, full stops and question marks. Through discussion, demonstration and activities, children should be encouraged to be aware of sentences both in their reading and writing. The considerable use of direct speech offers opportunities to look at the way speech marks help the reader to understand that someone in the story is speaking. Italicized sentences in *A New Home for Tiger* will help children to see how authors can add emphasis by presenting the text in different ways.

WORD LEVEL

The beautifully descriptive vocabulary of Joan Stimson in this story enables exploration of adjectives in the text, and investigation of new ones. As an active story, where Tiger 'bounces', 'swims' and 'pads', it also helps children to identify action words and carry out activities to consolidate their understanding of verbs. When illustrations and the text combine to lead the reader into a dramatic change of mood, there is an excellent opportunity to develop new vocabulary and phrases through brainstorming. Similarities in the text between the beginning and the end neatly draw a full circle to conclude Tiger's experience in moving home, and this allows for an investigation into many words and phrases which indicate time and how it has passed in the story.

READING THE TEXT

Note: The lesson plans refer to specific pages in the text, but since not every page of *A New Home for Tiger* is numbered, it is suggested that for easy reference you either lightly pencil in the omitted page numbers, or use small, numbered, sticky, removable circles.

To insure a fresh and uninformed initial study of the cover, it is suggested that the term 'Before reading' is taken literally for the first lesson plan. However, as a picture book, the story should then be read in its entirety, to enable children to enjoy and understand the full story. 'During reading' should be interpreted as studying the text in small sections while *re-reading* the story. Reading the blurb on the back cover has been deliberately left until the penultimate lesson plan, so that children can assess its relevance while reviewing *A New Home for Tiger.*

BIG BOOK

A Big Book version of *A New Home for Tiger* is available from Scholastic (ISBN 0-439-01172-8). This is an ideal resource for use in the whole-class sessions, as the teacher-led elements of the lesson plans which focus on the specifics of text and/or illustrations are made much easier to undertake through its use. Not only does the Big Book ensure that all children can see *A New Home for Tiger* properly but it enables the teacher to promote active participation and interaction with the text by the children. Most importantly, the teacher can use the Big Book for demonstration purposes. It also allows the teacher to draw attention to crucial details in the illustrations which the children might miss in their independent work, and to highlight points in the text over an acetate sheet.

ABOUT THE POSTER

SIDE 1

This side of the poster, showing a family with all their possessions moving home, enables children to explore ideas of what 'home' really means. It links with the underlying message of *A New Home for Tiger* that home is not just a building, but the place where the people we love, and all our familiar possessions, are. By discussing the poster, and looking for detail, children are encouraged to develop vocabulary relating specifically to homes, and house moves. By considering all the processes which are involved in moving house, children who may have experienced this are able to share their knowledge with others. Concurrently, children who have never had to move are prepared and informed for such an event. This analysis creates an opportunity for children to work on a group flow chart introducing the whole class to a method of sequencing ideas and actions.

SIDE 2

The poem 'Scuttling Spider' is used to link and develop the concept that '"home" can mean many different things' – a phrase used in the blurb on the back cover. It broadens children's understanding of the term 'home' to include the habitat of many creatures, and develops relevant vocabulary. The poem also encourages the study of patterns in poetry, and offers a chance to read a different kind of text with intonation and expression.

LINKED RESOURCES

OTHER BOOKS BY JOAN STIMSON AND MEG RUTHERFORD

Big Panda, Little Panda (Scholastic: Hippo)
Swim Polar Bear, Swim (Scholastic: Hippo)
Brave Lion, Scared Lion (Scholastic: Hippo)
Oscar Needs a Friend (Scholastic: Hippo)

OTHER BOOKS WITH A SIMILAR THEME

Let's Go Home, Little Bear by Martin Waddell and Barbara Firth (Walker)
Moving Molly by Shirley Hughes (Red Fox)
Mole Moves House by E Buchanan (Macdonald Young Books)
The Little House by the Sea by Benedict Blathwayt (Red Fox)

OTHER RESOURCES

Learning through Literacy: Homes by Jane Morris (Scholastic)
Let's Look at Animal Homes by Nicola Tuxworth (Lorenze Books)

LESSON PLANS

LOOKING AT THE COVER

RESOURCES NEEDED

Big Book version of *A New Home for Tiger* or an enlarged photocopy of the front cover, other books by Joan Stimson and Meg Rutherford (see 'Linked resources' on page 5), A4 paper, writing and drawing materials.

WHOLE-CLASS WORK

The aim of this lesson plan is to encourage children to look for information from the illustration and title in order to predict what the book may be about. Young children are often tempted to pick up a book and explore it, if the picture attracts them. The cover of *A New Home for Tiger* immediately acquaints the reader with the main character, but requires that the text is understood to fully anticipate the story.

A New Home for Tiger has a strong, appealing picture. Start by showing the children the front cover, with the title covered, and ask questions which will help them to look critically, seeking clues about the tiger's age, character and who else may be in the story. Would they like to meet this tiger? Whose tail is he holding onto? Why is he holding it so carefully? Have they ever seen any animals do this?

Next, uncover the text and discuss it. The title for this book gives the reader significant information about the possible contents of the story. But it is worth exploring the children's understanding of the term *new*. Is it a house which is newly built, or is Tiger moving to a different house which is new to him? This slight ambiguity appeals to the curious reader to find out more.

Now that they have seen the text and the illustration, can they predict what might happen to Tiger in his new house?

Talk about the author and the illustrator and look at other books of theirs. Discuss the fact that two people worked together to write and illustrate the book.

GROUP WORK

Organize the children to work in pairs. Ask each child to decide on the title of a story and write it on a piece of A4 paper. Encourage the children to look at other books to see the way titles are arranged on covers. Supervise groups which need help in formulating their thoughts and expressing them in writing. When they have each written a title, ask them to add their own names as authors, then exchange papers with their partners, so that each person illustrates the other's title for them. They should then add their own names again, but this time as illustrators. During this period, encourage each child to read and discuss his or her title with the illustrator, explaining what the story will be about.

EXTENSION

Children who complete their work early could use a computer to experiment with different fonts, sizes and emboldening for their titles.

PLENARY

Gather the groups together and from your assessment of the way the group worked, choose one of the following ideas for discussion:
✳ Look at some of the finished covers and ask other children whether they can predict the stories from them.
✳ Ask some children to talk about any problems they had in producing their covers with a partner.
✳ Did the authors feel that their illustrator had understood the title? Could they have explained it to them better?

LESSON PLANS

FACT OR FICTION?

RESOURCES NEEDED

Big Book version of *A New Home for Tiger* or enlarged photocopy of page 5, acetate sheet, books about tigers and other animals (both fiction and non-fiction), photocopiable page 21, flip chart or board, writing and drawing materials.

WHOLE-CLASS WORK

The first part of this lesson plan encourages children to look for features of fiction which distinguish it from non-fiction. Illustrations and style, and content of text are important indicators. So too are beginning sentences, and most children will appreciate that the traditional opening to *A New Home for Tiger* is an introduction to a story. We can use this understanding to develop their wider concept of fiction.

Before referring to *A New Home for Tiger*, start by saying 'Once upon a time there was...', then stop and ask the children if they have heard this beginning before. What sort of story usually follows this beginning? Will it be a true story? Will it be about giving information? Show them some of the other fiction books. Look at the illustrations and read the beginning sentences. Then introduce some non-fiction books and compare briefly the titles, beginnings and content, encouraging the children to note the differences between fiction and non-fiction. As the books are sorted and classified, place them onto a pre-prepared, labelled display to which children can return.

Now look at the first page of *A New Home for Tiger* and together read the text. Children will recognize the familiar beginning, 'Once upon a time...' For the remainder of this lesson plan, attention is focused on the description of Tiger contained in the first sentence.

Can the children tell you something about Tiger from the words in the text? Using an acetate sheet over the Big Book, ask if anyone can draw a circle around the words which describe Tiger. Some children may be unfamiliar with the word *tawny*, so give a description and show them an example. Can they think of other unusual words to describe colours? Looking at the illustration, can they offer any other words which would describe this tiger? (*Pretty, striped, cuddly, staring.*) List the words on the flip chart for use later in group work.

Can the children think of words to describe tigers and animals from the other books they looked at? (*Fierce, orangey, stealthy, hungry.*) Encourage them to appreciate that descriptive words help to give a picture of what the animal looks like or how it is likely to behave. Explain that descriptive words are known as 'adjectives', and the naming words like *tiger* which they describe are 'nouns'.

Studying the illustration, can the children think of any ways to describe the tail Tiger is holding onto? (*Big, striped, curling.*) Write the sentence 'Tiger has his paw on a long, stripy tail' on the flip chart. Can the children find the adjectives in the sentence? Point out that it is possible to have more than one adjective to a noun.

GROUP WORK

Place the children into differentiated groups and give each child a copy of photocopiable page 21, 'Describing Tiger', to complete the task individually. Explain that the task is to use words which most accurately describe Tiger in the illustration on page 5. Encourage the children to seek new words from the books on display, dictionaries and the flip chart.

✻ More able children should complete the whole photocopiable sheet.

✻ Less able children should complete the top section of the sheet only. Work with the less able group, ensuring that they fully understand the sheet, and the term 'adjective'.

EXTENSION

Children who complete the activity accurately could write a beginning sentence to add to their own title page from the previous lesson, using adjectives and a noun to correspond to their story.

PLENARY

Listen to some children reading their list of adjectives to describe Tiger. Discuss whether these new words suit the illustration in the book. If there is a general agreement, add them to the list on the flip chart, keeping the list for follow-up work. Other children may contribute further adjectives.

Children who have attempted the extension activity could read and explain some of their beginning sentences.

TIGER'S LIFE BEFORE THE MOVE

RESOURCES NEEDED

Big Book version of *A New Home for Tiger* or enlarged photocopies of pages 6 and 7, dictionaries, non-fiction books about animals, photocopiable page 22, flip chart or board, A4 paper, writing materials.

WHOLE-CLASS WORK

This lesson plan focuses on the illustrations and text on pages 6 and 7 to establish the setting of Tiger's life before the move. This will contrast later with his initial reaction to his new home. These two pages outline the basis of the story to come. The delightful similes applied to Tiger at this time are also discussed and developed.

Working first at text level, write on the flip chart 'Tiger's life before the move'. Explain to the children that this is what you want them to think about as they read pages 6 and 7 aloud during shared reading.

Ask some general questions about Tiger's life. Is he happy? How do they know, from reading the text? What else has the text informed them of? Discuss why Mother Tiger is excited. Does the *text* tell them where Tiger lives (that is, beside a lake)? When are they moving? Write some of their observations on the flip chart.

Now ask the children to look at the illustrations for other information which is not given in the text and has not arisen during the discussion. For example, some children may remember Mother Tiger's tail appeared on the cover, so now they know who it belongs to. Do they notice the caring way the tigers touch tails instead of holding hands? Does this tell them something else about Tiger's life? What do they think will happen in the new home?

In identifying text which gives an impression of Tiger's happy life, the phrases 'swim like a fish', 'eat like a horse' and 'slept like a dormouse' will attract the children's attention. Explain that these phrases are called 'similes', and encourage the children to consider their meaning. Children are sometimes confused by the literal meaning of similes and need many examples to illustrate that similes compare things which are alike in some way, but may be different in others.

Can they think of other similes they have heard, for example, 'as busy as a bee', 'as flat as a pancake', 'as soft as butter'.

GROUP WORK

Place the children into differentiated groups to work on one of the following appropriate tasks. Remind them to use the information on the flip chart as an aid, particularly for those children completing the photocopiable sheet.

✳ Ask more able children to use dictionaries and other books to make three lists of nouns based on the following headings:

Sea creatures
fish

Large animals
horse

Small animals
doormouse

✳ Suggest that an average ability group write their own ideas of other things Tiger might do in his present life.

✳ Work with children who need more help by giving them a copy of photocopiable page 22, 'Tiger's life before the move'. Explain that they should try to write their answers about Tiger's life in full sentences. Write 'Tiger's mother looked excited because...' on the flip chart, as an example for less able children to follow.

PLENARY

Look at the work from the second group – are their ideas relevant to the story's setting of Tiger's present life? Can anyone add more words to the lists compiled by group one?

EXCITEMENT AT MOVING

RESOURCES NEEDED

Big Book version of *A New Home for Tiger* or enlarged photocopies of pages 8 and 9, acetate sheet, dictionaries, reading books, photocopiable page 23, flip chart or board, A4 paper, scissors, hole punch, writing materials.

WHOLE-CLASS WORK

A New Home for Tiger is written in beautifully simple sentences which are ideal for illustrating the use of capitalization and full stops. This lesson plan starts by identifying sentences, and then looks at other ways to present text, for example in lists and labels. Some words from the text or lists are used to highlight the use of 's' to create plurals.

During shared reading, focus on the text on pages 8 and 9. Follow this by explaining briefly what a sentence is, and giving examples from the text. Ask more able children to read a sentence, individually and in succession, stopping at each full stop while the others follow the text with their fingers. Then ask a child who has not read to draw a circle around each full stop in the Big Book, over the acetate sheet. Show the children how, apart from the final one, each of these full stops is followed by a capital letter to start a new sentence. Ask another child to draw around the capital letters in a different colour.

Before learning to read, many children scrutinize illustrations for information about story content, and this is a skill which should be maintained, since illustrations help early readers to make sense of text. So now encourage the children to look carefully at the pictures on pages 8 and 9, giving them time to interpret the setting of 'moving day'.

Write the words 'Luggage list' on the flip chart. Ask the children to help you compile a list of things Tiger would have put into the bundles, for example *blanket, pillow, kettle*. Would any of these words be useful as labels for Tiger to tie onto the bundles to make it easier to find things at the new home? When the list is complete, help the children to identify those words which could be made plural by adding an 's'. Explain that the word *plural* means more than one. Can they find some plurals in the text? For example, *bundles, toys*.

LESSON PLANS

GROUP WORK

With children working in differentiated groups, choose the most appropriate task from the following activities.

✷ Work with able children who need to consolidate their understanding of sentences. Ask them to complete the activity on photocopiable page 23, 'Making sentences', using the flip chart as an aid.

✷ Ask children of average ability to use dictionaries and other books to compile a list of words which can be made plural by adding 's', writing its plural alongside each word.

✷ Invite less able children to make some luggage labels by folding and cutting sheets of A4 paper into four pieces, punching a hole at one end of each label and writing a suitable word on it; some labels can be written as single words, others as plurals using 's'. These children can use the text, flip chart or other sources for their words.

PLENARY

According to the needs of the group, select one of the following ideas to develop and conclude the work undertaken during group time.

✷ Discuss the new sentences the first group have made up. Do the others agree that these sentences describe the illustrations?

✷ Use the flip chart to write new words and plurals selected from the second group's list, and encourage the children to read them with you.

✷ Show the whole group some of the luggage labels, and later make them into a display by attaching them to suitable illustrations.

TIGER HAS DOUBTS

RESOURCES NEEDED

Big Book version of *A New Home for Tiger* or enlarged photocopies of pages 9–13, photocopiable page 24, flip chart or board, A4 paper, writing and drawing materials.

WHOLE-CLASS WORK

This lesson plan looks at how the text and illustrations on pages 9–13 reflect Tiger's doubts. Using the structure of the story may help children to think and write about their own experiences. Children may empathize with Tiger's feelings as he moves from a familiar to an unfamiliar setting, but like the character, have difficulty verbalizing their fears and doubts. Thinking about what Tiger thought, and said, is also an opportunity to draw attention to the use of speech marks.

Read the pages through together and then ask the children to focus on the illustration of Tiger on page 9, and the last sentence: 'He took a last look at the old house.' Can they say what he might be thinking? Have they ever felt like that? When?

Now ask them to read the text on page 10 and look at Tiger. Why is he lagging behind? Have they ever done this, and can they remember why? Has anyone ever told them to hurry up? When?

Write the words Mother Tiger is saying on the flip chart or board, explaining how speech marks help the reader to see when something is being spoken. Can the children suggest what Tiger might have said on pages 9 and 10? Draw a simple sketch of Tiger and draw speech bubbles which enclose two of their ideas. Show them how speech marks are a kind of mini speech bubble by 'converting' the speech bubble text the children have given into direct speech. For example, *Goodbye, old house* in the speech bubble becomes *Tiger said, "Goodbye, old house."*

Read pages 12 and 13, emphasizing the spoken words with a change of voice, while the children follow the text. Now ask them to identify the spoken words in the text by looking for speech marks.

Finally, the story is told in the past tense, using verbs with an '-ed' ending. Encourage the children to investigate this by reading the text from pages 9–13 again, identifying words which end in '-ed', for example *padded* and *whispered*. Write these on the flip chart. Ask a child to carry out some of these actions and explain the difference between *John is padd**ing** across the floor* (present tense), and *John padd**ed** across the floor* (past tense). Can the children think of any other examples (such as *jumping, jumped; clapping, clapped*)?

Goodbye, old house.

Tiger said, "Goodbye, old house."

GROUP WORK

Choose the most appropriate task from the following activities for children to work on in differentiated groups.

✳ Ask more able children to write about a time when they felt worried or afraid. They should work independently.

✳ Work on a copy of photocopiable page 24, 'What did Tiger Say?', with average-ability children, explaining each part of the sheet. Remind them to use the flip chart as an aid.

✳ Ask less able children to write an account of a time when they were told to 'hurry up' and to illustrate it in pictures using speech bubbles to show what the other person said and how they might have answered. This activity will reinforce their understanding of speech in text.

EXTENSION

Ask the children to read aloud the rest of the book, looking for speech marks and changing their voices to sound as if they are the character speaking.

PLENARY

Ask some children from the third group to show the class their pictures and read from the speech bubbles they have incorporated. Ask if anyone from the first group would like to say what they wrote about. Look at some of the completed photocopiable sheets and ask a child to read out the final section on what he or she would like to say to Tiger.

TIGER WANTS TO GO HOME

RESOURCES NEEDED

Big Book version of *A New Home for Tiger* or enlarged photocopies of pages 12–15, photocopiable page 25, 26 prepared cards (each with a letter of the alphabet on it), flip chart or board, A4 paper, writing materials.

WHOLE-CLASS WORK

Initially this lesson plan concentrates on using the text to develop understanding of the terms 'vowel' and 'consonant', by building on simple rhyming strings. Later the emphasis is on identifying and using questions in text.

Start by writing the five vowels a, e, i, o, u on the flip chart. Explain that these letters are all vowels, but all other letters are consonants.

Ask the children to work in pairs, reading the text from pages 5–15 and writing down any three-letter words which have a vowel in the middle and a consonant on each side. Write the word *put* (page 8) on the flip chart and ask if anyone found it. Ask three children to select these three letters from the alphabet cards. Can anyone identify the vowel? Now ask if anyone can change the beginning consonant to form a new word, for example *cut, rut*. Do the same with others from the text, building up rhyming strings and writing them on the flip chart.

Explain to the children that they are now going to focus on questions. Ask a few simple questions such as 'Has everyone got a book?' Return to the text, and ask them to look for a question on pages 12–15. Give them time to read and search the text individually, and then during shared reading, ask them to raise their voices slightly when they reach the question. Afterwards ask if they noticed anything which helps to identify questions. Draw a question mark on the flip chart and ask everyone to find it in the text.

Finally, look at the text on page 14 and ask a child to read the speech part. Can anyone think of a way to change Tiger's last sentence into a question? For example, 'Can I go home?' Can the children change any other text to questions which would be relevant, such as 'Don't you like it here, Tiger?', 'Would you like me to read you a story?' Are there any other questions which Tiger or his mother might ask at bedtime?

GROUP WORK

Place the children into suitable groups for the following activities.

* Work with more able children and those of average ability to role-play pages 12–15, where possible translating the text into question form. Help them to choose who will play which character (the elephant could be part of the role-play) and to make sure the story follows the structure that is given in the book. Encourage them to think about how Tiger is feeling as he enters his new home. What questions might he ask? Encourage the role-play groups to refer to the text but not be confined by it. Ask some children to act as observers, making notes which will enable them to report back to the whole class with a brief outline of the story as acted by the group they observed.

* Ask less able children to complete the activity on photocopiable page 25, 'Making new words'.

PLENARY

Ask some of the children who completed the photocopiable sheet to read from their lists of words. Recap on the work done on vowels, consonants and question marks. Ask some children from the role-play observers to use their notes to outline the story that was acted out.

TIGER IS GRUMPY

RESOURCES NEEDED

Big Book version of *A New Home for Tiger* or enlarged photocopies of pages 16–19, acetate sheet, dictionaries and reading books, photocopiable page 26, flip chart or board, A4 paper, writing materials.

WHOLE-CLASS WORK

A very important element of *A New Home for Tiger* is the way Tiger experiences the change in his life. Joan Stimson touches on many feelings which children understand, but may be unable to verbalize. This lesson plan looks at how Tiger's feelings and attitudes change in response to his circumstances and how the text and illustrations help the reader to follow those changes. It also investigates verbs and phonemes.

Following his initial happiness, excitement at moving, apprehension and then fear, Tiger is grumpy – a feeling which quickly turns to defiance and rebellion! Time spent re-reading the story together (up to page 19) to analyse why he has changed may help children to express not only Tiger's feelings but their own.

Look at the text on page 16 and focus on why Tiger is so grumpy. Why did he refuse to swim in the lake with the other tigers? Was this because these tigers were not friends from his old house but *new* tigers that he did not know? Why did he play with his food instead of eating it?

Encourage the children to see how the text and illustrations in this section of the book work so well together. Look at Tiger's facial expressions and how they reflect his moods. Draw attention to how his need to go home expresses itself. Finally, ask the children to look at page 19 and say how they think Tiger is feeling at this point in the story. Write some of the words and phrases they offer onto the flip chart and read them together.

Return to the text to discuss verbs. Explain that verbs are 'doing' words, and ask the children to scan through the story to find examples, such as *swim, eat, play, bounced, padded*. Write them on the flip chart under a heading 'Verbs'. Some children could act out these verbs. Ask the class if they know any other verbs.

Finally, investigate phoneme blends contained in the text to help the children with reading and spelling. Ask them to find the word on page 6 which begins with 'sl'. (*Slept.*) Can they find another word with the same beginning on page 13? (*Sleep.*) Explain how the two separate sounds 's' and 'l' are blended to make 'sl'. Write these words on the flip chart and add any others the children can think of that have the same beginning. Do the same with 'pl' (page 16 – *play*), 'sm' (page 25 – *smell*) and 'st' (page 9 – *stopped*; page 15 – *story*; and page 27 – *start*).

GROUP WORK

Place the children into differentiated groups to work on one of the following activities.

* Ask more able children to look at the illustration on page 16 and write what they think Tiger is feeling. It may help to have an introductory statement such as 'Tiger didn't want to swim with the other tigers because...' Work with this group, encouraging them to write in sentences and to think of more than one reason.

* Distribute copies of photocopiable page 26, 'Finding verbs', to children of average ability. Explain to this group that many of the verbs required for the cloze procedure, the first task on the sheet, will be found in the text.

* Ask less able children to work in pairs to find as many words with initial phoneme blends as they can. They should explore the text, and use dictionaries and other reading books.

PLENARY

Briefly discuss some of the suggestions about Tiger's feelings which have been highlighted by the first group. Write some of the phoneme blends, compiled by the paired group, onto the flip chart, emphasizing how the letters are blended. Finally, work through the first half of the photocopiable sheet with the whole group, allowing children to check their answers.

LESSON PLANS

TIGER MAKES UP HIS MIND

RESOURCES NEEDED

Big Book version of *A New Home for Tiger* or enlarged photocopies of pages 20 and 21, simple poetry books, photocopiable page 27, flip chart or board, tape recorders, A4 paper, writing materials.

WHOLE-CLASS WORK

Pre-reading children frequently 'read' books partly by remembering the story as it was told to them, and partly by making sense of the illustrations. This lesson plan makes use of these skills by encouraging children to read the text, look at the illustrations and then create some new sentences which are not in the text. Later, during group time, they are asked to retell the story in their own words.

Briefly remind the children of the previous pages, then carry out a shared read of pages 20 and 21. Ask the children to look carefully at the illustrations, and think of other sentences which could be added to the text, for example:

Tiger asked Elephant to help him.
Tiger put his luggage on Elephant's back.

What might Elephant and Tiger say to each other as they set off? Write some of the children's sentences onto the flip chart, for them to refer to later.

Now move on to exploring words in the text which rhyme. Point out to the children that two words on page 21 (*soon* and *moon*) have a similar sound, that they *rhyme* like some poems do. Ask the children to look at *mind* on the opposite page. Can they think of a word to describe Elephant, which would rhyme with *mind*? (For example, *kind*.) What other words have a similar rhyming pattern? (*Find, rind.*) Scan back through the text, picking on other words, such as *things* or *day*, encouraging the children to think of others that rhyme with them. (*Rings, wings.*) (*Pay, say, play.*) Write some of these patterns on the flip chart.

GROUP WORK

Place children into appropriate groups for the following activities and work alternately with the first two groups.

✻ Put children of different abilities into pairs – perhaps good readers with less able readers, or articulate children with those who need to develop their spoken language. Ask this group to first re-read the text on pages 18–21. Then they should cover the text and take it in turns to retell the story in their own words, using tape recorders. Remind them to look at the illustrations, and explain that they can add extra ideas of their own to elaborate on the basic story. Refer them also to the ideas on the flip chart.

✻ Ask some children to make up poems of their own, using some of the rhyming words on the flip chart, together with new ones.

✻ Ask less able children to work on a copy of photocopiable page 27, 'Rhyming words'.

EXTENSION

Invite children who have completed their group activity to look through some poetry books to compile lists of words which have rhyming patterns.

LESSON PLANS

PLENARY

Look at the illustrations on pages 18–21, while listening to one of the taped stories. Briefly discuss the differences of the children's version and the additions that have been made. Ask one of the children who has made up a poem to read it to the group. Finally, go through the activity on the photocopiable sheet, allowing the children who worked on it to check their answers.

CREATING ATMOSPHERE

RESOURCES NEEDED

Big Book version of *A New Home for Tiger* or enlarged photocopies of pages 20–25, acetate sheet, dictionaries, photocopiable page 28, flip chart or board, paper, writing materials.

WHOLE-CLASS WORK

This lesson plan looks at how the illustrations reflect change of mood and atmosphere – in particular at the way the darkening images on pages 20 and 21 lead the reader on into the atmospheric and dramatic pictures of pages 22 and 23. While the moon, the only colour in the darkening day, is still in evidence, the text tells of Tiger's determination and joy at going home, but suddenly, on page 23, Tiger's mood and body language change. He is *unsure* and *nervous*.

Start by reading through pages 20–23. Then ask the children to look at the illustrations. Ask them what they think about this part of the story. Do they notice the changes? How do they think Tiger is feeling? Can they see the difference between Tiger's bouncy body language on page 22 to that of apprehension on page 23? What is it that causes the change?

Encourage children to search the text for words or sentences which describe his mood, for example 'Tiger had made up his mind'. Ask a child to circle these on an acetate sheet placed over the page. Read on through pages 24 and 25, looking especially for clues to the change in atmosphere in both the text and illustrations, from Tiger's nervousness through to his sense that 'home didn't feel right'.

Now, through a brainstorming session, develop the children's ideas by asking them if they can think of other words and sentences which might create atmosphere. Tell them you are all going to make up another story. Ask them for ideas of who the main character might be, and what might happen. Can they think of new words to create a happy atmosphere (*sunny, playful, lively, friendly*) or a scary atmosphere (*dark, silent, creaky, frightened*). Write these words on the flip chart. Can they now put some of these words into short sentences? For example, 'It was a lovely, *sunny* day' or 'The cave was *silent*'. Using some of these suggestions, help them to structure a short story which moves from one mood to another.

GROUP WORK

Place the children into differentiated groups and choose the most appropriate task from the following activities.
❋ Invite more able children to develop an entirely new story within small groups, in a brainstorming session similar to the one carried out in the whole-class work. Very able children could scribe for the group, using large sheets of paper from the flip chart.
❋ Work with children of average ability to write individually their versions of the story produced during the whole-class brainstorming session, using the flip chart as an aid. Remind them of the work that was covered with the whole class and encourage them to include other atmospheric words of their own.

✱ Distribute copies of photocopiable page 28 to less able children and help them to understand what is required of them on the sheet. Completing it will help to reinforce their understanding of the text and illustrations.

PLENARY

Ask the children from the first group to share some of their ideas for stories with the whole class. Briefly discuss the advantages of the process of brainstorming for ideas. Review the photocopiable sheet with the whole class, checking for their understanding.

MOVING HOME

RESOURCES NEEDED

Big Book version of *A New Home for Tiger* or enlarged photocopies of pages 26–29, poster (Side 1), photocopiable page 29, flip chart or board, writing materials.

WHOLE-CLASS WORK

This lesson plan uses the text from pages 26–29 to interpret an essential message from the story, that home is where the people we love are, and that they, and our familiar possessions, are what really make a home. The poster reaffirms this message, using Side 1 to investigate the idea that a house move for people involves moving all the people and possessions which make up that *home.*

Start by reading the text of these pages together, noting the change in the illustrations as Tiger moves away from the dark pages of confusion and doubt and into the warm, light illustrations of his return home and his realization of what *home* means. Use the flip chart to write for emphasis the sentences from the text which crystallized his understanding:

Tiger felt confused.
Then he realized what was wrong.

Ask the children if they know what it was that he suddenly realized.

Move on through the text, drawing attention to the words and sentences which are italicized. Ask if anyone knows why this has been done. Explain that this is to add emphasis, making sure that the reader understands the importance of this text. On page 27 it is as if Tiger *shouts, 'I want my home!'* and when reading aloud, the voice of the reader might be raised.

Now look at Side 1 of the poster and encourage discussion of the picture. Help the children to look for details and associate the items with their own home and possessions. Draw attention to the vocabulary, and ask the children to read it from the poster.

Ask the children to think about all the processes which are involved in moving home. Point out the 'For Sale' notice with 'Sold' placed across it. Can they think why people decide to move? Some children may have experienced a house move, and will offer reasons such as 'needing more room', 'change of job', 'bigger/smaller garden' and so on. Take them briefly through the process of what happens next – that is, estate agent, buyer, packing, removal men – making notes on the flip chart.

GROUP WORK

Place the children into differentiated groups and choose appropriate tasks from the following activities.

✴ Work with more able children, in pairs or small groups, to produce simple flow charts of a house move, using sheets of paper from the flip chart. Where possible, include some children who have experienced relocation. Spend a little time showing the children what you mean by a flow chart, and remind them of the sequences discussed when looking at the poster. Show them how to start from the beginning with a 'decision to move'. Finish by briefly comparing the charts for similarities and differences.

✴ Ask the other groups to complete a copy of photocopiable page 29, 'Moving home'.

EXTENSION

Invite the children to work at a computer to write further sentences from the text which include italicizing. Can they find other sections of text which they would like to italicize? Alternatively, they could write out the sentences by hand, using bold colour instead of italics.

PLENARY

Select children who worked on the flow charts to talk through one of their charts. Review the photocopiable sheet with the whole group while children who completed the sheet check their answers. If any of the children completed the extension activity, ask one or two of them to read aloud some of their sentences, emphasizing the italicized parts.

FULL CIRCLE

RESOURCES NEEDED

Big Book version of *A New Home for Tiger* or enlarged copies of pages 4, 6 and 30–32, dictionaries, similar text-level fiction books, photocopiable page 30, paper, scissors, glue, staplers, writing materials.

WHOLE-CLASS WORK

This lesson plan begins by looking at the similarities of the text in the final part of the story pages (30–32) to that at the beginning (page 6 and the small illustration of Tiger on page 4).

Help the children to draw conclusions from these similarities, such as 'Tiger is happy again, he has settled into his new home, made new friends and everything is back to normal'.

Then, in order to develop their understanding of time in stories, remind them that a lot has actually happened in the story since the beginning. How much time do they think has passed since the beginning of the story? Look through the text as a means of assessing this. Read together phrases such as:

"I've found a new house for us and tomorrow we must pack up our things."
Early next morning, Tiger put his toys in a pile.
And night after night he woke Mum.

The answer will not be conclusive, but it will establish that it was not years, but most likely a few days or weeks. Encourage the children to confirm this by looking at the illustrations – that is, Tiger still looks the same; he has not changed or grown up!

Look, too, at less obvious references to time:

At last they were ready to leave.
"Hurry up, Tiger," called Mum, "or we'll never get there."
"I'm going home now," he announced.
As soon as the moon came up...
"It's time to tuck me in," he shouted to Mum.

Open a discussion on everyday terms we use for time – for example *night, day, evening, morning, breakfast time, bedtime*. Can they think of others?

Now consider time in relationship to sequence – what happened when? Briefly recap with the children the main events in the story. Start off by saying, 'At the beginning of the story, Tiger was a cheerful tawny tiger. What happened then?'

GROUP WORK

Place the children into differentiated groups and choose appropriate tasks from the following activities.

✴ Work on photocopiable page 30, 'The story of Tiger's new home', with more able children. Explain to them that they are going to make a shortened version of *A New Home for Tiger* by putting the illustrations into a sequential order of events from the story.

✴ Encourage average-ability children to work together to compile a list of all the sentences in the text of *A New Home for Tiger* which reflect time passing.

✴ Invite less able children to research the text of *A New Home for Tiger*, dictionaries and other books to compile a list of words related to time.

PLENARY

Scan the text of *A New Home for Tiger*, identifying again the sentences and words relating to time. Make a class list of time words, including those found by children in the third group. If time allows, ask one or two children from the first group to share their sequenced stories.

LOOKING AT CHARACTERS

AFTER READING

RESOURCES NEEDED

Photocopiable page 31, flip chart or board, paper, scissors, glue, writing materials.

WHOLE-CLASS WORK

This lesson plan encourages children to review the story of *A New Home for Tiger*, and to look carefully at the characters.

Through shared reading, re-read the story. Briefly recap the basic outline of the story and ask the children to give their opinions on it. Did they enjoy it? If so, why? Which parts of the story appealed to them most? Would they recommend it to a friend?

Now read the blurb on the back cover. Explain that when choosing a book from a shop or a library, this is what readers often look at first because it gives clues as to what the story is about, and helps them to decide if they will like it.

Do the children think that the blurb of *A New Home for Tiger* would have made them choose the book? Is it accurate? Would they change it in any way? What would they include or omit?

A New Home for Tiger has only two main characters, which makes it ideal for children to scan back and consider the relevance and importance of the two personalities. Ask who is the *most* important. Could the story have been told without anyone else but Tiger?

Draw attention to the elephant. What was his role? Can they offer any words which would describe him, for example *strong, heavy, large*? Write these words onto the flip chart as a list. Now ask for antonyms which would describe a character that was the exact opposite of Elephant, for example *weak, light*. Explain that some words have more than one antonym, such as *large/small, tiny*. Where appropriate, write additional antonyms opposite the first list.

Scan the illustrations together to look for details. Mother's tail played a significant part in the early pages, but do the children notice the toy buffalo on pages 6, 8, and 14? Do they think this is Tiger's favourite toy?

Throughout the text, capitalization has been used for Tiger and for Mum. Point this out, and illustrate how the children, too, use capital letters for their names. Using their surnames as examples, can they think what Tiger's surname might be? And his mother's name? (Mrs...) Briefly explain that they also have a formal means of address, Master or Mistress, later to become Mr or Miss/Ms/Mrs.

GROUP WORK

Organize differentiated groups to focus on one of the following activities.

✳ Ask more able children to look back through the illustrations, and write a story about the elephant and how he helped Tiger and his mum. They should use a range of strategies to check their spelling, from the text and dictionaries.

✳ Invite children of average ability to write their own blurb about *A New Home for Tiger*. Encourage this group to refer to the text for ideas and vocabulary but to aim to find their own style.

✳ Work with less able children to use a copy of photocopiable page 31, 'The elephant's story', to create a story about Elephant. Some children may find it easier to cut out and paste the pictures onto a separate sheet first.

PLENARY

Look first at examples of the completed photocopiable sheet, asking one child to read his or her short story to the rest of the class. Ask one of the more able children in the first group to read out their story. Finally, discuss briefly one of the blurbs written by the second group.

HOME CAN MEAN MANY THINGS

RESOURCES NEEDED

Poster (Side 2), acetate sheet, a selection of poetry books, two sets of prepared cards (one set with the names of the creatures mentioned in the poem on them, the other with pictures or simple sketches of their homes with which to match them), photocopiable page 32, display board, paper, writing and drawing materials.

WHOLE-CLASS WORK

This lesson plan takes up the phrase on the back cover of *A New Home for Tiger* – '" home" can mean many different things...' – and explores it through poetry.

Start by reading the blurb on the cover of the book and ask the children what they think this phrase means. Remind them of the work covered in the lesson plan 'Moving home' (see page 16) and of the things which make a home. Then explain that the right home for some creatures will be different from others.

Read the poem 'Scuttling Spider', on Side 2 of the poster. Ask the children to look at the poem and name some of the homes mentioned and who lives in them, for example *web* and *spider*. Organize the children into pairs and give out a set of matching cards to each pair – for example *bird* and *nest*; *rabbit* and *burrow*; *frog* and *pool*. Read the poem through again, all together, and with expression. Emphasize the paired words, and encourage the pair holding each set to raise the cards at the appropriate moment. Afterwards, display the cards on the board for reference.

Now spend a little time looking at the rhyming patterns in the poem. Ask the children which ones have a similar sound. Explain that in poetry, words can sound similar, but are not always spelled the same, for example *motion/ocean*. Word endings which have the same vowel and final consonant or consonant cluster such as *small* and *wall* are called 'rimes'. Ask an able child to circle the words which rhyme on an acetate sheet placed over the poem. Using these circled words as a guide, illustrate that in this poem the pattern is to match the last word of the first line with the last word of the second line in each verse.

Draw attention to the use of alliteration, for example *scuttling spider; shiny, slippy, slimy snail*. Can they think of any other examples, which aren't in the poem, for example *tawny tiger, brown bear*?

Look also at the descriptive words in the poem. Ask the children to find the words which describe the creatures mentioned, for example *bright-eyed; long-eared*. Explain that sometimes description relates to the movement of the creature as well as its appearance, as in *scuttling spider; leaping frog; blindly tunnelling tiny mole*.

Read the first verse to the children again, emphasizing the rhythm and beat, then ask them to read it with you in the same way. Encourage them to read the next verse in a similar manner.

GROUP WORK

Choose the most appropriate activity for children to work on in differentiated groups.

✴ Ask more able children to refer to the poem to write and illustrate a series of simple sentences as follows:

> A spider's home is a web.
> A bird's home is a nest.

✴ Place children of average ability into pairs and help them to find and make a list of alliterative words in poems contained in a selection of poetry books.

✴ Distribute copies of photocopiable page 32, 'Home can mean many things', to children who need to enrich their vocabulary and sentence structure. Remind them to use the poem or cards as an aid when they are completing the sheet.

PLENARY

Ask some of the children who worked in pairs on the second activity to share some of the alliterative words from their lists. Then ask selected children from the first group to read out some of their sentences. Finally, review briefly photocopiable page 32 with the whole group.

Name _____   Date _____

DESCRIBING TIGER

✳ Look at the illustration of Tiger in the story, and draw your own illustration.

> Draw Tiger here.

The story describes Tiger as **cheerful** and **tawny**.
These words are known as **adjectives**.

✳ Circle the right adjectives from the list below to make a list of other words which also describe Tiger.

| small | cuddly | angry | spotted | green | stripy | pretty | ugly |

✳ Can you add some more adjectives to describe him?

_____

The sentence at the beginning of the story is 'Once upon a time there was a cheerful, tawny tiger.'

✳ Write this sentence again, but use two new words to describe Tiger. Choose from the lists above.

_____

_____

✳ Now write a sentence to describe yourself.

_____

Name _____   Date _____

TIGER'S LIFE BEFORE THE MOVE

✸ Read pages 6 and 7 and look at the pictures. Then answer the questions.

Why did Tiger's mother look excited?

_____

_____

_____

Where is Tiger's new house?

_____

_____

_____

Similes

Tiger could swim <u>like a fish</u>. He could eat <u>like a horse</u>.
The underlined phrases are called **similes**.
Choose the right words from the box to complete the similes.

| puppy | needle | snow | mouse | giant | coal | tortoise |

as slow as a _____   as tall as a _____

as white as _____   as black as _____

as quiet as a _____   as playful as a _____

Name _____   Date _____

MAKING SENTENCES

Every sentence should begin with a capital letter.
✳ Put a circle around all the letters which should be capitals, and put in a full stop at the end of each sentence.

early next morning Tiger put his toys in a pile

he bounced round Mum and helped load the bundles

at last they were ready to leave

a little way along the track Tiger stopped

he took a last look at the old house

✳ Make up some sentences about the illustrations on pages 8 and 9.
Remember to use capital letters and full stops.

_____

_____

_____

Plurals
Write the plural for each word in the list. The first one has been done for you.

kettle _____kettles_____   toy _____

tree _____   bundle _____

tail _____   track _____

Name _____   Date _____

WHAT DID TIGER SAY?

Tiger is going into his new home for the first time.
✳ Write in the speech bubble what you think he might have said.

Speech marks are put around words to show readers what is being said in the story. They look like this " ".
✳ Put speech marks around the words which are being said by Tiger.

It's all different, he whispered after supper. Can I sleep in your bed? he asked Mum.

✳ Here are some sentences which are not in the story. Read them carefully and then put in the speech marks in the right place.

Put your toys in a pile, said Mummy.

Tiger stopped. I just want a last look at the old house, he said.

Yes Tiger, you can sleep in my bed, said Mummy.

✳ Think of something you would like to say to Tiger and write it below. Remember to put in speech marks.

_____

_____

Name _____   Date _____

MAKING NEW WORDS

These letters are all **vowels**:   a   e   i   o   u

✸ Draw a line to match words which have the same vowel in the middle. One has been done for you.

hat   bud

get   dog

fit   cat

log   sit

mud   wet

All the letters below are **consonants**:
b c d f g h j k l m n p q r s t v w x y z

✸ Add a consonant to the beginning of these letters to make a word. Make words that are in *A New Home for Tiger* – or think of your own!

___ut   ___un   ___um   ___an   ___ed

✸ Some of these sentences are questions. Put a question mark like this ? at the end of each sentence you think is a question and a full stop . at the end of the others.

This is fun   Can I come with you

Are we ready to leave now   It all looks different

Name _____   Date _____

FINDING VERBS

✻ Look at the story of *A New Home for Tiger* to help you find the missing verbs in the sentences. Remember that verbs are words which tell you what someone is doing.

Tiger _____ through the doorway and _____ inside.

"Can I _____ in your bed?"

He refused to _____ in the lake with the other tigers.

He began to _____ with his food instead of _____ it.

One day Tiger _____ up his things.

✻ Now choose the right words from the list of verbs in the box to fit the sentences below.

cooked	brushed	cleaned	kicked	played

The boy _____ the ball.

Geeta _____ the dinner.

Jodie _____ the car.

The baby _____ with her toys.

The girl _____ her hair.

RHYMING WORDS

✱ Read the words under each picture on the left. Draw a line to the picture opposite which has the same rhyming sound.

✱ Write the correct word under each picture on the right. One has been done for you.

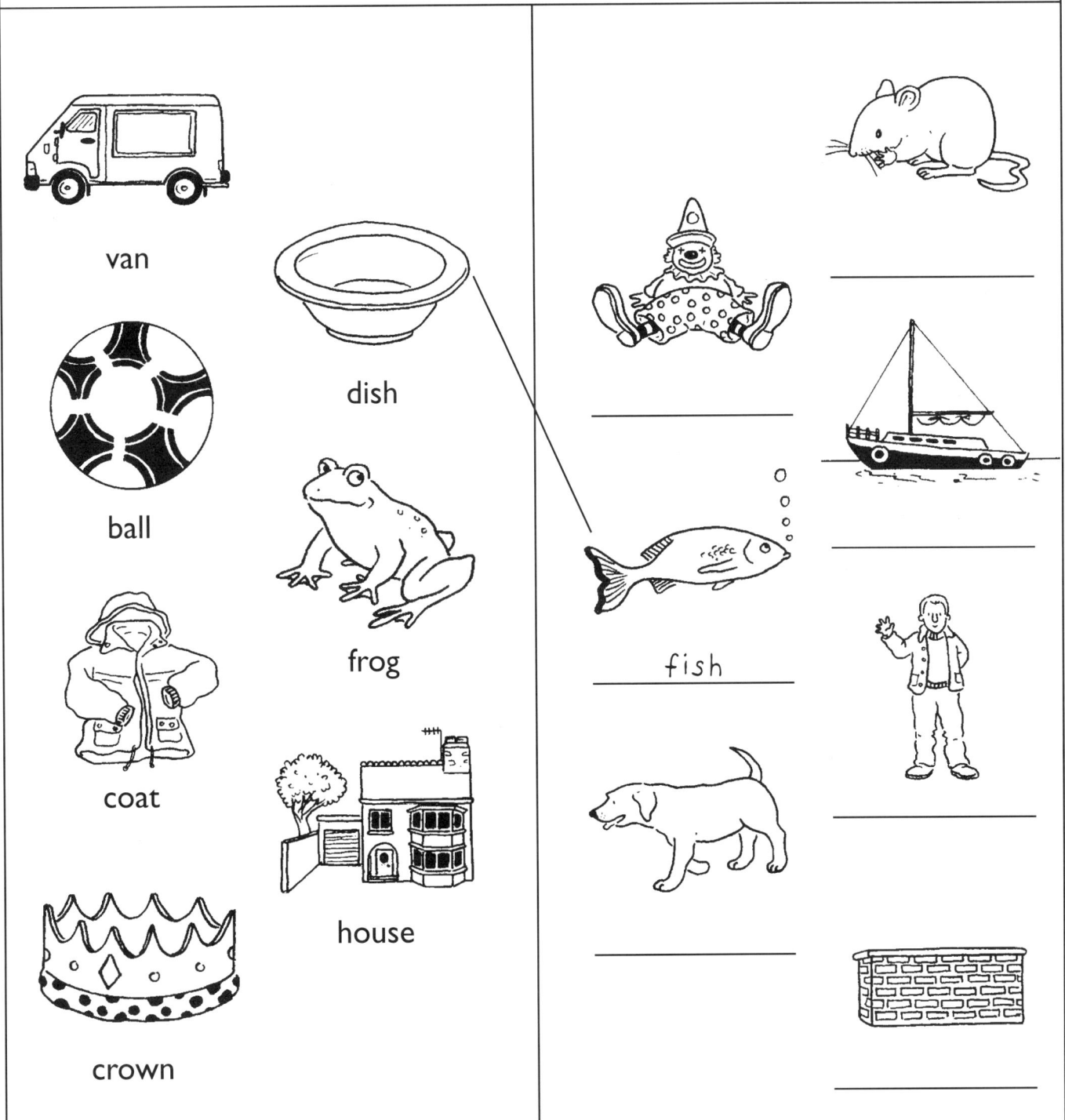

van

ball

coat

crown

dish

frog

house

fish

Name _____   Date _____

TIGER'S MOOD CHANGES

✸ Here are two illustrations of Tiger. Look at them carefully, and think about how Tiger may be feeling. For each picture, choose words from the box to describe Tiger's mood and write them underneath it.

happy	excited	nervous	scared	frightened
cheerful	playful	unsure	lonely	pleased

1.

2.

_____   _____

_____   _____

_____   _____

_____   _____

✸ Finish the sentences. Write about Tiger in picture 1, then write about Tiger in picture 2.

Picture 1   I think Tiger is _____

Picture 2   Tiger is feeling _____

Name _____   Date _____

MOVING HOME

✹ Match the words to the pictures. One has been done for you.

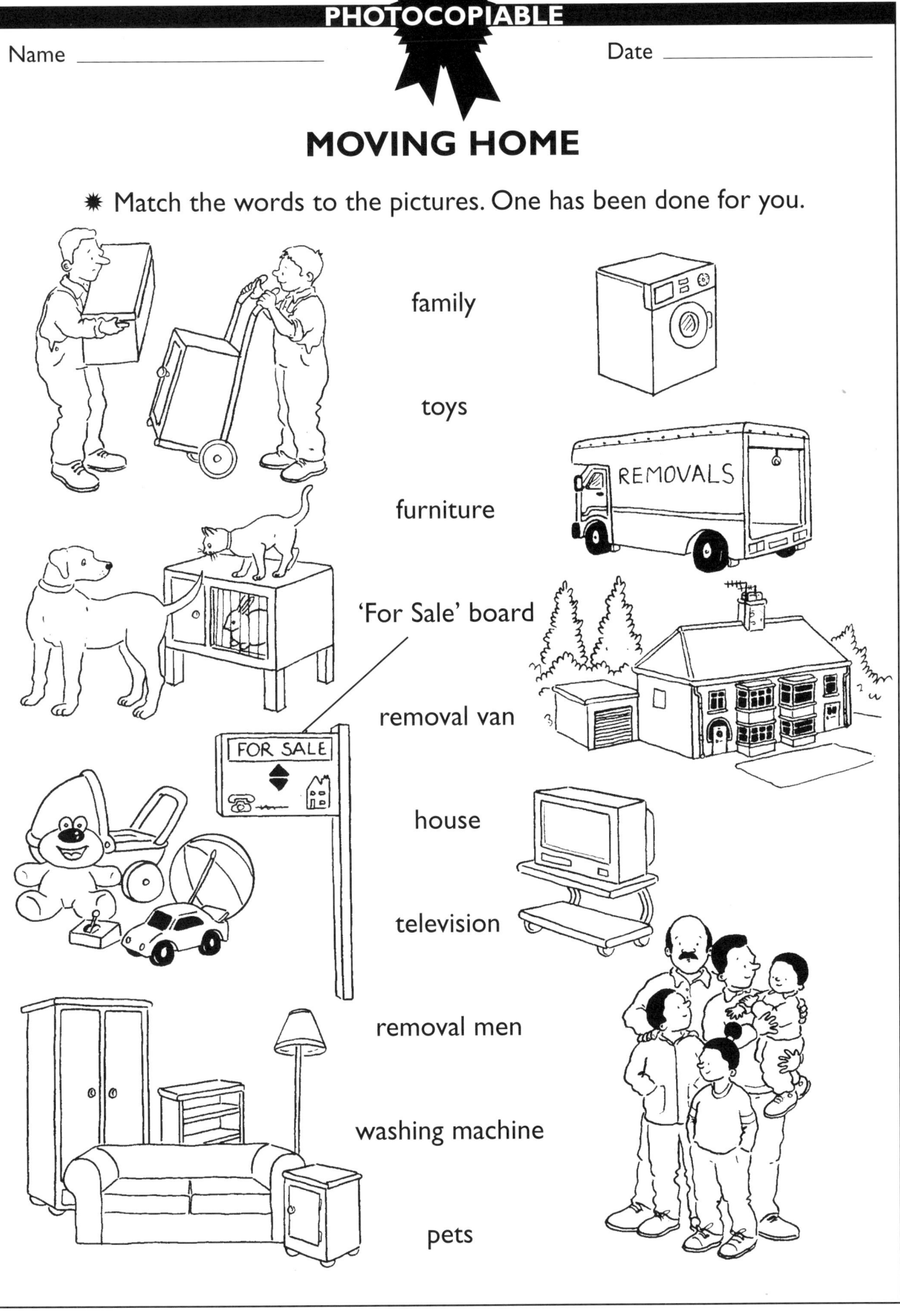

family

toys

furniture

'For Sale' board

removal van

house

television

removal men

washing machine

pets

Name _____   Date _____

THE STORY OF TIGER'S NEW HOME

✳ Tell your own short story about Tiger's new home. Cut out the pictures and glue each one onto a sheet of paper.
✳ Write a short sentence underneath each one, place them in the right order, and staple them together to make a little book.
Don't forget to write the title on a page at the front!

PHOTOCOPIABLE

Name ____________________ Date ____________________

THE ELEPHANT'S STORY

✷ Look at these pictures carefully. There are similar ones in the story *A New Home for Tiger.*

✷ On a separate sheet, write a short sentence for each one, so that together the pictures tell a story about the elephant.

Start your story with picture number 1, then 2, 3 and 4.

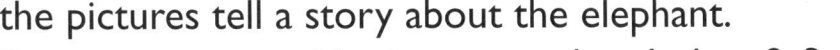

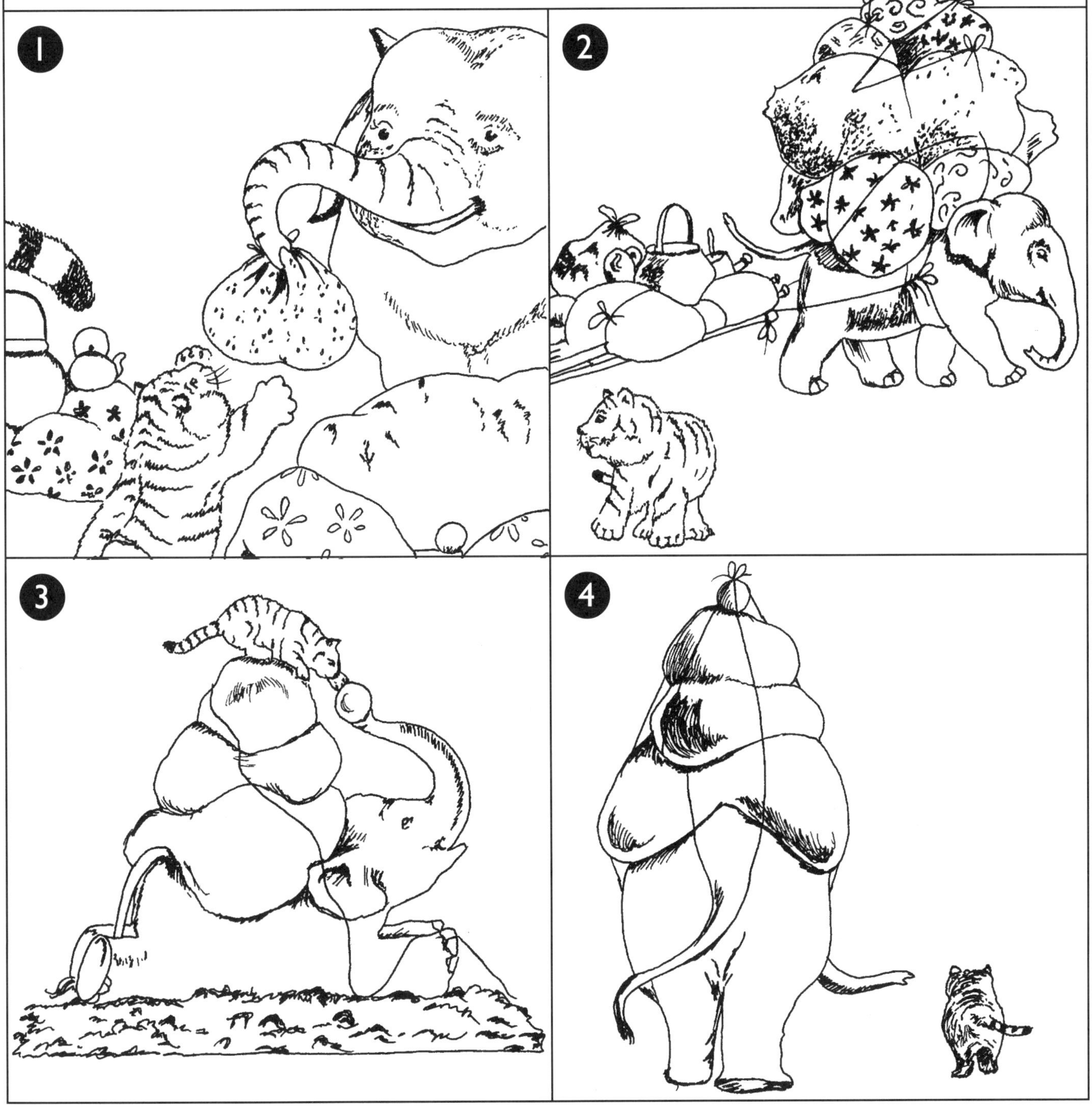

Name _____   Date _____

HOME CAN MEAN MANY THINGS

✳ Draw a line from each creature to lead it to its home.
Remember you can use the poem to help you.

hole

whale

shell

rabbit

pool

spider

burrow

nest

snail

ocean

bird

frog

web

mole

✳ Use some of the words above to complete these sentences.

A _____ lives in a _____

A _____ lives in a _____

A _____ lives in a _____